Enjoy Your Business

Aphorisms for passionate can-doers

by Matthias Scharlach

Copyright: © 2018: Matthias Scharlach
Umschlag & Satz: Erik Kinting
www.buchlektorat.net
Cover picture: © Halfpoint, fotolia.com
Back picture: © xavier gallego more, fotolia.com

Publisher:
tredition GmbH
Halenreie 40-44
22359 Hamburg

Dedication

By: _____

For: _____

We want these sayings to inspire you. Discover
new horizons!

There may be thousands of books dealing with various questions on successful management in a serious way. That ist very important, of course. Although I am convinced that a good many things even in this field could be taught much easier by humorous learning.

The present booklet contains sentences and maxims on management in form of aphorisms.

It intents to inspire reflection on business matters by smiling.

It does not claim completeness which is boring.

Matthias Scharlach

Everything can be arranged more or less ingeniously in different ways. I preferred the following division for the contents of this booklet:

Fundamentals   7

About Customers, the Market and the Marketing   29

About Colleagues   33

About Managing and Being Managed   42

On the Organization of Labour and Responsibility   66

How to Deal with Time   80

About the Organization
of One's Own   91

About Creativity,
Quality and Efficiency   106

On the Strenghts and
Weaknesses of Characters   119

A Bit of Ethics   131

Go into business   144

Fundamentals

Management is - to organize the realization of one's own ideas by others in a sensible way.

Only the future can be managed.

A strategy always begins with knowledge about the real matter.

Strategic management is sense of reality looking to the future.

Top managers are good
information processors with good
informers on their side.

Just as the management is the
brain of a company the
acquisition is its heart.

Bankers can be anything but
entrepreneurs.

Controlling is concrete
supervision in business.

Statistics is the pornographic
aspect of economic
mathematics.

A company can subsist on
capital, labour and distribution,
but it cannot survive on them.

Knowledge and competence are
the catalysts of success.

Any fusion is like a wedding, at
which the children by one's first
marriage are brought along.

Integration is always a question
of profitability and not of
company size.

Regulations are changeable
rules of a game.

Regulations are rules of a game
which often lead to more games.

Each goal needs a scale.

Problems are the motor of each
development.

Money-making starts if you can save time.

A managing director is a man who - to some extent - is also paid for being guilty.

The half-life of a managing director is directly proportional to his company's success.

Stairs do not only lead upwards.

Management Consulting should have an effect like a dash of rum on top of a sugar-loaf:
After full penetration of the upper level the distribution to the lower departments follows.

The best way of controlling is the practical checking.

Most literature on management
seems to have been written by
zoologists who deal with the
training of highly developed
primates.

Success has three dimensions:
cost, quality and the feeling to be
on the market at the right time.

Innovation, readiness for taking a risk and skills are basic requirements in order to have a good start for running successful companies.

Continuous profit - that's superior business.

The market is the entrepreneurs' playground.

Marketing is world-outlook
through customers' eyes.

The path into self-employment is
the metamorphis from the
customer to the customer
consultant.

One, who does not keep talking
to his customers, will soon have
noone to speak to.

If you want to be innovative you should be able to listen to your customers.

If a customer is talking to you, it is in your own interest that he knows that you are sure what you are talking about.

Cheap work is of small value.

One, who treats customers like guests is wrong.

The work done by a salesman consists in the clever selling of others' results.

Real and imaginary advantages of products are sold to the customers.

In order to sell useless products splendid advertisments and silly shoppers are needed.

Somehow, we all are customers and we do not want to be disillusioned.

It is much better to call needs and to control change than to recognize needs and to calculate change.

A need is always the desire for a solution.

To discover real needs in our perfect world - this is the road to success.

Economy is based on demand. Marketing above all is work with the human-being.

A marketing concept needs to be in touch with the customers.

Not everything which marketing staff knows is also revealed by them.

On the way to the end user there are expensive middlemen.

If a dealer says to you that there is nothing to make money out of any longer then it is high time for an investment.

It is like practising mysticism if you try to read an economic forecast from the point of view of a "simple" high-school student.

We often rack our brains about conclusions and forget to think if the assumptions are right.

A good marketing department
and a madhouse have one thing
in common:
they are crawling with obsessed
people.

Representatives represent the
show-business of a company.

Competence is the highest value
in competition.

To be competitive in a double sense means for a manager to keep harmony between his daily routine and his strategic decisions.

Our competitors are our best partners.

There is enjoyment in change which is the seismograph of a firm's culture.

Constructive change is the source of successful business.

A company gives identity to its employees.

There are fashion styles also in business.

There is method even in madness.

An entrepreneur is a slave who is permanently forced to do something in order to accumulate.

Money is transferable power.

Money changes objectives into liabilities.

There is no petting in business.

Practical industrial management above all means to teach tax evasion.

Overtaking is more expensive than driving down another lane.

Everything is all right as long as it goes wrong.

About Customers, the Market and Marketing

There are "Supernova"-markets:
They expand rapidly like an
explosion with immense
luminous power and afterwards
they become "black holes".

Several companies have an
effect like large pink balloons.
A pinprick will do and there is
nothing left over.

"Blooming" companies are always somewhat closer the fading than newcomers.

Over and over again there are companies which survived their entrepreneurs - and vice versa.

On principle, there is nothing human within a company - besides the fact that it needs human-beings.

Conservative management goes
to the market to feel threatened.

Chances fall by cashflow.
There are no stupid jobs but
stupid people in all walks of life.

About Colleagues

There is nothing more valuable for a clever manager than his colleagues.

Each group of people works out its own dynamic force - sooner or later.

Some colleagues are like white cabbage. If you put pressure on them, they will become sour. But sauerkraut is good.

People whose work done only consists in criticism are "money-swallowing" obstacles to innovations.

If your colleague has got a problem, make himself solve ist.

One's pride develops in individual problem-solving.

A problem belonging to your colleague is dealt with care by him.

If your boss roars, you should not show that you notice his uncertainty in him.

Discipline is the wisdom to act in such a way that your boss takes pleasure in it.

A boss can be a psychologist,
his his staff must be
psycholgists.

Imagine your boss naked in the
desert. If he still makes an
impression on you, you should
keep working for him.

Loyality can also be an
expression of laziness.

There is a simple philosophy of employees:
If you pay, I will work hard.
If you pay more, I will work harder.
If you do not pay, I will be off.

There are colleagues who do exactly what they are told to do - and not a little bit more.

Working is much harder in paradise.

If your colleague only does what
he is told, it is his tactful hint at
his intention to leave the firm.

One, who does not love his
work, should get divorced from it.

There are white collar workers
who seem to be paid according
to the quantity of their problems
and not to the success of their
work.

Sometimes salary is related to merit.

There are co-workers who get too much money only for their co-work.

A controller who only catches input - output operations has the intellect of a cash-register.

Diligent fools are the worst of all.

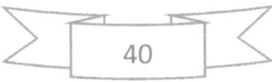

Colleagues' problems tend to be driven upwards to the management department.

The best working conditions are useless if there are not pots of gold.

About Managing and Being Managed

Management is action forged on
life experience.

To manage departments is an
activity - to manage people is a
skill.

Managers are catalysers in the
production of ideas and
concentrater of social energies.

You cannot practice good
managing without cunning.

A manager is a person whose
result depends on the efforts and
the ability of his subordinates.

A manager is always expected to
do more than a single person is
able to do.

A secure position may lead to conservatism.

There would already be progress if only people who can really manage something called themselves manager.

He, who believes that companies can be managed with figures and not with people, will soon get his notice.

It could be very useful to control controllers.

As a manager you gain experience, make enemies and cause envy.

He, who boasts of his rank, is nuts.

Conferences of managers are meetings of individualists and should be chaired by psychiatrists.

The self-complacency in business management is a kind of active euthanasia.

Each entrepreneur has that management which he deserves.

Each management can be
looked at by three points of view:
by a bookkeeping one,
by a legal one and
by a sensible one.

Each general manager who was
put in the position of a "creative
soldier" by his partners is
actually an "executive zombie".

He, who is not participating, just
participates poorly.

A managing director, who is only a bookkeeper, is not a manager in any case.

If you want to improve something you should correct the course which led to an unsatisfactory result - but you should not "recycle" the result.

An objective is always something you can reach - everything else is fiction at best.

Before staking on profit viability
should be guaranteed.

You must be able to recognize
the main connections in order to
do all the little things properly.

Each proramme is as good as
the will of the chairman.

It is easiest to replace one chaos
with another.

If a living organism dies, at first
the head smells bad.

It requires stressful collective
stupidity in order to save a
company to death.

In a purification plant the
consequences of slipshod
working habits can be taught in a
very material way.

Increase cannot be ordained; it comes from inside.

The best companies function like a good family.

Modern leaders are creative managers but no sacred gurus or madmen craving power

That boss is respected who demands top performance, promotes personality at the same time and sets himself a good example.

A clever manager employs people who are cleverer than he is.

There are as many solutions for the efficient employment of the staff as there are colleagues.

Good experience can be improved.

Initiated self-management is the "high" school of chief-management.

90 per cent of coaching consists in the selection of the right person.

A good managing style makes a
good working style possible.

A manager is not a headteacher:
He does not give marks.

An instruction should begin with
putting oneself in the position of
the instructed person.

He, who faces poor results
conciliatory, behaves like a
smoker on a petrol barrel.

As long as people who are never
inproper get the best mark for
their behaviour all remains in
vain.

Open achievement tests are the
best way to cause deep distrust
of the management.

You can charge a person with a problem:
... in order to cause a necessary activity, ... in order to strengthen his self-confidence or ... to prove his incapacity to solve just this problem.

Before delegating work you should be sure of the "receiver's" willingness and ability.

If a person informs you of something, the most important question ist: Why does he do this?

The low tones are the most effective ones.

Each motivation begins with respect for the personality.

He strangled himself by his own lines of reasoning.

If you want to work with creative people you must allow mistakes.

Most people genius have been killed by boredom.

There is nothing worse than the degradation of a creative person by charging him with daily routine.

It is always good to be near people who permanently prevent you from doing something wrong.

You are really good only then
when you are respected by
others without the roundabout
way through their awareness.

He, who wants to act in a far-
sighted manner, must be aware
of short-sighted people.

If administration is inefficient it
need not be the staff's fault.

Big companies need their undercover agents in order to be able to calculate the underground movement in administration.

He, who thinks he could manage efficiently by a strict hierarchy, suffers from a profile-neurosis.

You will have to pay dearly if you do not look after your fellows.

Confidence is the oil in the gearbox of management.

We fly to other planets but we are afraid to go the path to other people's heart.

Executives who cannot talk to their subordinates should be locked up or immobilized by money.

A boss' greatness can be valued
by his sensitivity to criticism.

Managers who treat their
colleagues in an overbearing
manner should be quickly made
aware that they have been
overbearing.

He, who believes in the good
side of the human-being must
also be able to go through hell.

He, who wants to be promoted to a higher position, should have brought up a worthy successor.

If you want to get to know something about your boss, have a look at his junior staff.

On the Organization of Labour and Responsibility

Each new path you follow begins
in your thoughts.

What matters is: to have always
more ideas than you actually
need.

Each manager has a small case
of ideas which are to be
recycled.

Not the precise perfectionists are successful in business, but the pragmatists taking a risk.

You cannot expect from a manager that he likes graduates.

Analysts think "quantumly", seldom in a global way.

A doctor helps to put humans-beings, a manager - to put companies on their feet again.

Before you start working you should know what to do.

Sometimes there is a relation between success and work.

If you know your employees' trade, it is impressive. If you do their work, it is stupid.

The best way to "managing harakiri" is the effective settlement of other people's tasks.

He, who works like two workers, should dismiss one.

If all colleagues are responsible for everything, nobody will be responsible finally.

A manager who believes he could replace his colleagues with himself is efficiency-mad.

If you take over responsibility from others, it often turns out to be an expensive luxury.

If your colleague tells you that we have got a problem, do ask him why he speaks to himself or to you as a third person.

Control is good, responsibility is better, to control the ones responsible is best.

Responsibility is the scourge of the honest people.

Managers who are loyal to their companies sacrifice the Queen in order to save the King.

He was so dynamic that he - owing to his sheer energy - did not reach his aim.

Mediocre people slap their backs at that time when experts start working.

Success is a "child" of
perseverance.

Networked thought does not
necessarily mean entangled
thought.

Not every matter needs the
same degree of order.

It is better to trip over bagatelles
than to struggle against them.

If something is always done in the same way, it can be a good tradition or the expression of incapacity to make it better.

We must learn to deal with contradictions and not to avoid them.

The four stages leading to real
management are:
- Do it yourself.
- Delegate work.
- Coach your employees.
- Supervise.

Superficiality is the "En-Terrible"
of flexibility.

Most companies still work on the
principle of enlightened
absolutism.

Fixed dates are the "icons" of good organization.

All matters which are highly important are the boss' concern; all important matters are fixed in his pad; all urgent things are the colleagues' concern and the rest is thrown away in the wastepaper bin.

We learn to forget information which we intend to keep safe for later since we do not need it at the moment.

Thinking should precede speaking.

The most important part of a conference, certainly, is not the opening welcome.

Only the richest companies can afford an official car for the boss without a chauffeur.

He, who wants to make money quickly, needs cheap co-workers.

How to Deal with Time

Time has its own geometry. You can follow its ups and downs.

Management needs time.

The secret of success consists in the distribution of work.

A manager who does everything himself is going to have nothing to do soon.

There should be a good lock on
each door which leads to the
boss.

The more you do the less is
finished.

There is a difference:
to work in favour of your
colleagues or to do their work.

There are different types of
managers:
the ones who let no grass grow
under their
feet to do the right things,
others who do a lot at a time and
such who kill time.

You can pass your time with
work or you can also do a
splendid job.

He, who does not manage his work, will not manage to work.

A long-term task takes a long time.

A good time-management begins with well-aimed coaching of the colleagues.

Good questions save time.

Also very old things have their time.

Free time for thinking is the vital nerve of innovative companies.

The greatest stupidity of an entrepreneur is to take away spare time from his colleagues.

Spare time is a tender plant
which is to be cultivated in order
to grow.

Time is life.

If there is too little time to
develop reasonable views, you
must demand.

Children have a great dislike of
doing something at once.

The bosses, who are really irreplaceable, are the ones you do not miss because of all that work.

Self-management begins with reaction that leads to involving of others.

A manager needs three things: ambition, devotion and discipline.

A manager is a kind of
purposeful clever chameleon.

He, who behaves like a
"mimosa" in business, will not be
able to stop twitching.

Think it over:
Everything changes a bit every
day - including you.

Not everything you can do you
should actually do.

The greatest virtue of an
entrepreneur is his ability to call
himself in question by inqiry.

An entrepreneur stays young by
challenging as well as by looking
for challenge.

Success means to put through
one's ideas.
That which is change for
someone is chaos for others.

Only castrated cats live without
stress.

About the Organization of One's Own

It is not enough to be an optimist - you should also be a realist.

Some people mix up positive thinking with successful displacement of unpleasant facts.

Do always speak about what you are for - against what you are is being noticed without saying.

Laughing is music for the soul.

The intelligence to live is more valuable than the intelligence to grasp a theory.

Only the one who comes to terms with himself has got the necessary harmony for success.

Most problems are caused by ourselves.

He, who cannot explain a problem within five minutes, creates another problem for himself.

You cannot wish to solve a problem you are not aware of.

The ones who never have problems are gossips.

Each problem is a chance to do something better.

This man is competent who knows all arguments in his field and who can evaluate them.

The most important learning objective is to use one's brains.

Real understanding starts if you do it yourself.

Well-being is a state of
successful prophylaxis.

The ones, who are straight
arrows do not like to bend easily.

Good intentions can prove fatal
under poor circumstances.

Honesty only makes sense if you
deal with honest people.

If you work successfully but your boss mistrusts you permanently, your boss does not deserve you.

If you do not like your boss' wishes; change them.

To speak to your boss' wife about the company is at least boldness.

Our experience is nothing else but events which we digested easily or badly.

It is at least stupid to consider experience always in connection with time-honoured age.

Not everything which is obvious must be right, too.

Believe in your intrinsic values but not in human-beings.

Thinking becomes complicated when you know little and when you know too much.

There is a kind of "brain-guard" sitting in your head and putting the deluge of information on the active or passive side of our brain.

Logical thinking is only one kind of thinking.

Brooding is the panic of thoughts.

The heart of the matter lies between pleasure and frustration.

It is easier for you to climb if you have touched on the ground before.

The higher the bar, the easier you can dodge under it.

A men who feels he could pull out whole trees by the roots should now and then try his hand at a couple of shrubs.

You can only be tolerant from a
firm point of view.

Some managers are lucky:
They can face both business and
share holders in a loyal way.

Do never what your competitor
expects from you.

It is a feat to wind one's way through life without becoming a worm.

You should work in order to feel good and you should make your money work for you in order to live.

He, who dips in the cookie-jar, will soon be running on empty.

If you cannot do anything, do it with a serious face at least.

Our adjectives lose value if we use them only to express soft soap.

Why do harm to the language? You can also say nothing with the help of simple words.

There must also be matters you cannot reason with your manager about.

About Creativity, Quality and Efficiency

Genius is an ability to solve a problem simply.

Creativity is the sister of unselfishness.

What are all averages, tendencies and trends compared to the feeling of being able to deal with concrete things and facts?

Innovation is the achievement of irrational people.

Innovation is vision which has been realized in a sensible way.

A good manager needs the attraction of contradiction.

If you are surrounded by yes-men, your creative life will be finished.

To follow the fashion means -
not to have imagination.

Dilemma starts if you suffer from
a lack of imagination.

You should not only think a
matter over but more often you
should think of it beforehand.

Plenty of knowledge is too little.
It must be of high value.

You should also learn to exchange ideas.

Our knowledge is like a magnet. It attracks problems and new ideas.

Whoever has the "perfect" solution is imperfekt.

Mere logic is the death of each creativity.

If a conclusion does not produce a contradiction, it need not mean that it is really true.

For some an idea can be the first rung of a ladder - for others already the complete ladder.

Already the manner in which a question is asked separates the wheat form the chaff.

The best people are in doubt about their results in a most creative manner.

You can work too much but you can never achieve too many results.

Not work and efforts are interesting but achievement and results.

An ability comes to light only in connection with performance.

If you want to be better than others, do not freeze in respect for others' results.

The best are not the ones who go round as plagiarism of their teachers.

If you can prove that a matter is
good and essential, you should
put it through even if the sceptics
wore white beards.

Quality is always the result of a
proof.

Quality begins with
accomplished prophylaxis.
Quality is a fundamentally
subjective matter first of all.

The death of all creativity is if
you follow advice permanently.

Each pattern is a coffin for
thoughts.

A manager should be able to
play.

You can achieve something new
with the experience of age and
the unreasonableness of youth.

A bad result is a result, too.

Grey eminence subsists on prestige and not on performance.

There are people who are in panic fear of novelties because their motor follows a circular course and does not follow cycles.

The officials' humor expresses in grinning about unconventional thoughts.

It is inhuman to tell an official something about creativity.

Sceptics, know-alls and grumblers are the best motivation for every creative person to go his own ways unperturbedly.

Masters are successful and say even the truth.

He, who is expected to achieve top results, has a right to get the best management.

The real ingenious solutions have often been based on error.

On the Strenghts and Weaknesses of Characters

A real entrepreneur distinguishes himself not only by striving for success but above all by courage to hold out.

Peace of mind and certainty are the basis of management.

He, who has character, has also difficulties.

A human-being has got a spine,
a personality a backbone.

Modest people are often quite
remarkable.

The answer to the question why I
support a matter is the
motivation for success.

Also bosses need tenderness.

Sometime it is relaxing to let oneself drift if the direction is right.

Some people smoke a pipe only in order to have a toy if they need time for thinking.

Too much soberness is more regrettable than too much emotion.

The ones, who do not wonder at anything else, should not belong to the management.

Life on earth is a daily degradation for managers who declared themselves gods.

Working for fame leads to believe that not any more the performance but the straightest way to a medal is most important.

The ones who aim higher but who are not able to achieve it often act on the "principle of relative quality".
They put the others under pressure in order to seem more powerful.

Standard managers who can adapt themselves are important. They care for stagnation and regression stages of development.

Regressions cannot be done
away with depressions.

Most people are in positions -
driven by a mistaken view of
their career - in which the victory
of a gastric ulcer over their skills
is predestined.

There are not few people who
are not capable of moving under
the weight of their own official
position.

Some people mean really what
they say.

He, who always tries hard to say
"right" things, has already done
the wrong.

He, who always agrees, is
careless.

Sensitive people give advice to other sensitive people not to be so sensitive.

Be careful:
the "indispensable" people do not have successors.

Occasionaly you meet verbal revolutioners who live in a world of words and nonactions.

When his firm was going to be ruined he was talking about the luminous power of the "tail" light.

Over and over again it is breath-taking how cooly intellectuals behave who - with great difficulty - managed to create a sixth sentence where there were only five.

Directors of museums and archaeologists often talk about "what could have been".

He did not work any more. He only designed his image.

There should be directors who always express their own lack of understanding in their branchmanagers' words.

There are situations which are too much serious in order to mope around.

Even managers have got a gall-bladder.

A Bit of Ethics

Is a philosophy all-powerful because it is true or is it true because it is all-powerful?

World has not become better or more reasonable by the technical civilization but more complicated above all.

You can buy reasonableness.

The stupidity of most people is stronger than their common sense.

Only the stupid person and the clever one get ahead - the others feel annoyed at the unpleasantness of life.

Intelligence must always overcome the bounds, whereas foolishness is without bounds.

Thoughts are free - as long as they remain thoughts.

Our words are echoes of thoughts.

The value of a conviction is that you cannot buy it.

You cannot manipulate convinced people.

After two million years of mankind history we managed to live in a world of trivialities and noble stupid things.

The dilemma of this world is the "human" society.

If there should exist an economy in future, it must be based on environment and not on money.

The ape became a human-being by work and the human-being again turned into an ape by money.

Money can replace intelligence, personality and morality.

He, who controls money, is the ruler about good and evil.

Our society is a society of "To Be and To Have".

Design determines consciousness.

Today it is not only different to the past but also many things are new.

A real entrepreneur is always a materialist.

Politics is nothing les but
struggle for power.

Economy acts, politics describes
the objectives.

The merry-go-round of
knowledge, money, power and
weakness is called democracy
by politicians.

The road to power is the history
of mental rapes.

People with a "good conscience"
often know nothing about a
matter.

Mighty people provided laws in
order to get justice under control.

After social changes at first the intelligence will be paralysed. And what is left?

Morality is the virtue of the have-nots and the luxury of the rich.

Also the hyena has got morality.

Cream and scum swim on top.

Also the unchangeable realities are created by people in most cases.

To follow rules without thinking - this has claimed the most victims among people.

Knowledge is the spring-board of the mind.

Those who look for enlightenment will have to climb down from the top of the hill to the valley of effervescent life.

The absence of knowledge has a power more dangerous than that of knowledge.

Mass of people feels better in the high tide of successful people.

The human-being is a pigheaded
creature; he always places
himself in the centre.

Sometimes we discover practical
philosophy which already the old
Greeks nodded about
thoughtfully - and we are so
bold, too, to keep nodding.

Go into business
Some friendly advice
for newcomers

In a seminar on corporate communications, a friend of mine, a journalist, said, "You see, I have been studying so hard, I know quite a lot that others don't know and I work all day. Nevertheless, on of my classmats who is a businessman can afford much more than I can. What's wrong with what I do?"

I said to him, "I am sure you are a very efficient journalist, but as a businessman you do quite a few things wrong. In your profession you produce, present and sell information. To earn 'good money' you must pull off the right coup and pass on news of high interest and rarity value. You must not only know your job excellently but also be able to wait for the right opportunity.

If you don't like this and look for another job, you should first ask yourself two questions: Which occupation will make me personally happier? And: Will I be able to stand it practically and morally?

Making money is basically not a matter of sophisticated intellect.

Only with dealings of the 'elevated type' the intellect is brought into play as the additional 'swirl of cream'.

Money making is essentially a trade which is founded on skills, experience and intuition - often even on the preliminary work of ancestors.

So, for one thing, journalism and business activity are differently structured, which does not mean that at a later stage the former should not be effectively reconcilable with the latter.

If you have decided to go into business to amass 'real money' though you don't dispose of major financial means to start off with, you should understand the interaction of four items:

- Work -
is the playground man has chosen to counter the environment his way.
In most cases it's more valuable than it's price. As a trader of this 'surplus value' you will gain advantages.

- Capital -
is work accumulated in objects of value. If you want more of it, use it along with additional work to speed up the production of further objects of value.

- Land -
understood as the relatively constant human sphere of life, is the best thing for any businessman to possess. Water, air, ground and other property are among the vital 'foodstuffs' of man.
The person who owns this kind of land 'has' the people, too.

Banks always regard land as their
ultimate goal.

- Man -

ist a child of nature, the producer of work
and the vehicle for capital increase.
Before money can work man must first
have produced capital. Every man strives
for survival and under the conditions of
private enterprise, the preservation of his
species takes second place only.
Economically he is as valuable as his
capacity for work required on the market,
or rather as his catalytic effect on the
increase of value.
You can exchange this value on the
market: for capital, other workers and
land.

What do you own? What are you worth?

You have your body and your mind.

You are able to work and learn, you have special knowledge at your disposal and are highly motivated.
What else do you own? A flat, a car and some money in the bank - so, nothing worth mentioning.

How can these possessions help you to get yourself some money?

1. The world of capital ist the world of the self-employed, it is not that of civil servants and employees.
If you want to become 'self-employed', first and foremost act that way.
Find out your strong points, develop your own ideas and concentrate persistently on what you are particularly good at.

2. Be productively suspicious.
Don't trust in anyboldy except yourself.

Asses your fellow men - even your partners and friends - at their actions, not at their words.
Test advice for it's consistency befor following it.

3. Remember: Learning is a specific form of work and know-ledge a specific form of capital.

4. Use your knowledge, your working power and will to
influence relationships consistently:
- relationships of owners of land and/or capital to you,
- relationships between owners of land and/or capital,
- relationships of owners to their land and/or capital.

5. Make strict use of your knowledge and skill to change these relationships in your favour. But do not take away

anything from those who own property and/or capital. They would fetch it back and they are still more powerful than you are. A good deal is always a matter of problem solving for all those involved.

6. Do not aks more than those you want to manipulate can afford, but do ask.
Let them keep the illusion of being privileged.

7. Make use of other people's working power to carry out your ideas.
Pay them a fair price for it so that they can develop their skills and remain motivated to work for you. However, never pay the real amount of their work's market value, for just this difference is the source of your wealth.

8. Be egoistic without demaging the environment.

This kind of egoism is morally respected as an expression of the self-confidence of the mature citizen both by progressive businessmen and the society.

Greedy egoism is respected by businessmen of conservative caliber but publicly despised by the society. This will delay your progress.

9. Learn to cope with defeats, to carry on in periods of misfortun, to overcome the unforeseen , to blaze new trails towads your goal again and again - but never give up.

10. Consider the fact that the world you want to conquer is inhabited by people who reckon with men like you are."

About the author

Matthias Scharlach was born in Germany in 1950 and spent his childhood and adolescence there. After finishing school and completing a locksmith's apprenticeship, he studied to become a certified teacher of mathematics and physics, worked as a teacher, and then focused on researching personality psychology. He spent several years as a university lecturer, wrote doctoral theses, and had work published both within Germany and abroad. In 1989, he became a professor, and founded a university institute for educational sciences. The emergence of personality tests and assessments saw him move fields, at the age of 41, from the university sphere to the free economy, where he has since been running seminars on management training, change management, the development of personal core competencies, and career planning. He fell into prose

unintentionally through his various encounters and stimulating discussions with different political, business and cultural figures. His aphorisms are thus smile-inducing "distillates" from his observations of human behavior in decision-making and challenging situations. They invite readers to reflect and improve. Designed as a smart giveaway, his "Enjoy Your Business" booklet features a collection of sayings on the manifestations of those "all-too-human" things.

His life philosophy is "Do things with enthusiasm and commitment, or don't do them at all!". Matthias Scharlach is happily married with two sons. He loves good food in a stylish setting, but can just as easily spend a couple of weeks slumming it in the wilderness. He is constantly fascinated by foreign cultures, interesting people, adventures and the art of problem-solving. His favorite authors are Raymond Chandler and Jonas Jonasson, and his favorite painter and sculptor is Bruno

Bruni. He likes the music of Dire Straits and Maurice Ravel.

Zeitfracht Medien GmbH
Ferdinand-Jühlke-Straße 7
99095 Erfurt, Deutschland
produktsicherheit@kolibri360.de